COURAGE
REFLECTIONS AND LIBERATION FOR THE HURTING SOUL

COURAGE

**REFLECTIONS AND
LIBERATION FOR
THE HURTING SOUL**

NGINA OTIENDE

Published by Intentional Today Books.

Copyright © 2023 Ngina Otiende

All rights reserved. This book may not be reproduced in any form, in part or in whole or by any means electronic or mechanical, including storage and retrieval systems, without the explicit written permission of the author.

Scriptures taken from the Holy Bible, New International Version®, NIV®. Copyright © 1973, 1978, 1984, 2011 by Biblica, Inc.™ Used by permission of Zondervan. All rights reserved worldwide. www.zondervan.com The "NIV" and "New International Version" are trademarks registered in the United States Patent and Trademark Office by Biblica, Inc.™

ISBN: 978-0-9986892-2-7

This publication is intended to provide helpful and informative material on the subjects addressed. It is not intended to replace the advice of trained healthcare professionals.

Cover and interior design by Emmalee Shallenberger.

To the courageous ones.

Table of Contents

Patriarchy	2
His Dignity Held	4
Burning Heap	6
Song of Liberation	8
Permission to Unpeel	10
True Freedom	12
Sisterhood: I Am with Her	14
Her Strength	16
Safer	18
Church Escape	20
Fraudulent Religion	22
Abuser god	24
In His Image	26
Not a Mistake	28
Her	30
She	32
The Rupture	34
Love Is	36
Culture	38
Wifehood Is Not a Death Sentence	40
Watch Out	42
Silenced Prayer	46
Goodwilled	48
The Baseline	50
Peeling Away	52
Co-Regulating with Christ	54

The African Lament: Home	56
The Choice	58
About the Author	61
Notes	63

WHY THIS BOOK

A few years ago I began addressing some of the adverse experiences I had that arose out of living in a country and culture different from the one I grew up in. I was born and raised in Kenya, but I have lived in the United States for over a decade. What I didn't know was that I was tagging at a wispy thread of a well-worn sweater: everything that could unravel would unravel. Childhood trauma. Religious trauma from harm suffered in the different spiritual spaces I had occupied. Trauma from a chronic condition that has hounded me for years. My body had been waiting for a sign that it was safe to put down the burdens it had been carrying for decades. And unburden it did.

One of the things that goes out the window in seasons of unrelenting stress or triggered, unprocessed trauma is our mental, emotional, and physical bandwidth. Our capacity to hold focus for long, to linger in diverse thoughts, or retain multifaceted information goes by the wayside. This was true for me as I began to write what became this book, and I imagine it has been or will be the same for you at times as well. Therefore, this book is intentionally short. It's simply poetry. My hope is to help you untangle lies and cling to truth in gentle, affirming steps. Please allow yourself to read, linger, and write notes at a pace that feels feasible to you, however slow that might be.

As I journey through life in a female body, I am persuaded that women who accept the invitation to see themselves as image bearers revealed in the person of Christ, who is Emmanuel, God with us, must first tap into something else within themselves: courage. The word "courage," when it is attached to a woman, is not a favorite thing in patriarchal circles.[1] However, it is an invitation for women who want to thrive as God created them to. Courageous means, "not deterred by danger or pain; brave."[2] Courage encompasses passion, tenacity, wisdom, hope—and a firm grasp of truth in the face of any opposition. Courage such as this drives a pulsating conviction that men and women are equal and that we were created to work together on equal footing.

"But Eve was named by Adam" is one of the many refrains regurgitated by those who use religion to justify the subjugation of women and girls. Such people deploy verses like Genesis 2:23 as mic-drop proof texts to rationalize why they believe man is superior to woman and that she was created to bow under his "authority."

It is indeed true that the author of Genesis records the man's response to seeing the woman for the first time: "This is now bone of my bones and flesh of my flesh; she shall be called 'woman,' for she was taken out of man."[3] Many have decided those words mean women belong to men, that it is an announcement of male superiority, instead of seeing Adam's words as an observation of physical fact. "This is at last bone of my bones and flesh of my flesh" proclaims connectedness, equality, and mutuality, not dominance or a hierarchy of power.

I write these words to those who have been told to take their place in the valley of desolation: those who thought they were free but still carry the burden of male superiority and classism on their shoulders; those hurt by wolves dressed in sheep's clothing; those walking through life with a broken, disjointed soul. And those who love them.

I call you courageous. Fierce. Beloved.

My prayer is that Courage: Reflections and Liberation for the Hurting Soul will inspire you to peel off the lies that cling to your skin like Lazarus's burial clothes. I hope these words help you to embrace who you already are. May you find your seat at the table of courage and belonging and feel affirmed to continue taking steps that align to your true, authentic identity as a daughter of God.

Applauding you,

Ngina

Poetry

Patriarchy

They said, "patriarchy is in the Bible,"
"it's here to stay,"
"it's the godly order,"
"deal with it."

Of course,
patriarchy is in the Bible.
So is rape.
Multiple wives.
Idolatry.
Sexual immorality.
Slavery.
Incest.
Orgies.
War.
Greed.

The bleakness of these.
Not many argue divine permission.

Just because it's in the Bible
doesn't mean it's instructive.
Just because it was formerly
doesn't mean it is presently
meant to be modelled after.

Patterning our lives after Christ
is supposed to be our daily breath.
Not proof-texting Bible verses
to justify the broken veins
He healed and freed us from.

Not a few verses
taken out of context and misinterpreted
should silence everything else
the Good News has said.[4]

Your Thoughts

His Dignity Held

*I am struck by how many women work so hard to
"submit" to their husbands or to male church
leaders who are merely adolescent boys
in men's bodies. These are men who demand to
be "respected" yet do not live "respectably."*
—Andrew J. Bauman[5]

Males with total authority over women,
submission received but never given,
never sat well with us.

But along we went.

Chaffing at the unending indignity,
stuffing, denying, and minimizing sacred feelings.
We made a home in the gully of "the Bible says so."

We made a home: Until that day when
Truth welled up.

Like a swell in the ocean, indiscernible at first,
Then rising, whooshing, and impacting the shoreline,
Truth saturated every barren place.

We never stopped being in His image
even when they told us we were lower.

He never stopped being our Liberator
even though they said He didn't liberate that much.

We may have imbibed and regurgitated
the words, the "theology," biases, and persuasions,
often to explain away the discomfort
and questions.

But Truth always had a home in us.
Something in us never bought into the landfill
that was the marring of us.

Our gut knew, our bodies knew,
our spirit knew.
Because the Creator created human beings,
both male and female, with a map
and vision of dignity deep in their souls.

Your Thoughts

Burning Heap

Their whole world didn't collapse
into a giant flaming heap.

They didn't sit in the ruins
wishing to wake up from a smoking
pile of a nightmare that wouldn't end.

They don't know the pain of
unanswered questions,
a howling silence from heaven,
the odors, wrinkles, tastes
of a faith and hope incinerated.

So they wouldn't know of a Savior
who sits in the ruins without demands,
hurry, or reproach. A Savior sitting still,
remaining as you flail against His steady
arms and cooling streams.

Inspecting a corrosive, disembodied
Christianity and finding something
beautiful and meaningful in the ruins
will look like foolishness and losing faith
to the watching folk, who are complicit in
their silence and neutrality.

But your faith-from-the-ruins,
though noxious and sulfuric to some, is
evidence of your holy rising, your fierce
blade of truth, emerging from the flaming
heap of what was into the blazing glory of what is
and will be—is your strength and legacy.

Your Thoughts

Song of Liberation

Those familiar with birthing freedom
rejoice in another's song of liberation.

They stared down their strongholds
and wrestled with darkness,
cried for His presence, wondering
if He heard at all.

They crawled through the tunnel of
a gritty, unceasing train barreling through
the night, longing for a flicker of illumination,
the evidence of daybreak stealing in.

Finally fastening their eyes on the first shaft of bronze
beginning to paint the dark walls outside the window
of the long train rumbling under the earth,
the tension down in their bones, as the brush of bronze
grew, chasing away the shadows of the moon until
finally falling out of the belly that kept them safe
from the dangers that lurked in the darkness
and held them captive
from the beauty that was around them.

Those who've birthed freedom,
whose flesh is intimately familiar with the steel bones
of the all-night train, know freedom is sweet
and scary.

So they lift up another song of liberation
for the one journeying through the tunnel,
the one emerging from the belly of its protection,
the one chasing away its confinement.

Your Thoughts

Permission to Unpeel

Some versions of Christianity teach us to
distrust our feelings and war with our bodies.
To silence our voice and numb our pain.
To stuff our hurt and "spiritualize" body and earth.

So when a relationship has tipped over the edge
and left you lonely and mashed up,
like a strawberry dropped from a car in motion,
skewering in the blazing heat of an eager sun,
at the mercy of the elements and the next set of
wheels, you still can't tell you've been hurt.

**

Here's to the script-flippers.

Who refuse to ask permission to unpeel from the
hot asphalt. Who refuse to seek approval before
they shade their souls and pursue peace and safety.
Who understand old minds put up a fight and so
accept every messy middle as the path to existence
and health.

Here's to truth-huggers.

Who know it to be true that the Good Shepherd
is not in a hurry to "fix." There's no medal for
the person with the least amount of questions
or the lowest decibel of pain.
No awards for keeping it zipped up and tidy
as you fall off the edge and crush to the ground.

Here's to awareness.

That developing empathy for ourselves
is a healthy step forward,
not an unhealthy step backward
to unbelief.

Truth be told, unbelief is also normal
when in the past "truth" has been used
as a weapon.

Health and clarity for your life and marriage
looks like a nurtured, growing capacity for wisdom
and discernment to make good decisions.

A pastor, friend, or family who appoint themselves
gatekeepers of your clarity and discernment, who
stay neutral and peddle circular talk, who see
gentleness as an enemy of healing, who contend
harming spaces are important for your progress,
who will not hold space for your messy middle,
are the ones paddling in the wrong direction.

Grant yourself permission to unpeel
from the hot burning asphalt of their
opinions and intimate presence.

Your Thoughts

_____
_____
_____
_____
_____
_____
_____
_____
_____
_____
_____
_____
_____

True Freedom

Emotional drivel and thundering words by
a pastor about "deliverance from dead, cold
religion," supposedly into life and freedom.

Quite the contradiction
coming from the king of the castle
who rules with an iron fist
in a high-voltage evangelical kingdom.

Isn't it soul-shredding to hear the shouts of
"Liberation" while living in controlled,
orchestrated reality.

To hear "God's people are free"
while the crack of shackles rings in your ears.

To sit under words, habits, and systems
designed to keep you hindered.

God's people walking on earth, thinking they are free,
imprisoned in a version of reality far from real.
To question the thundering shepherd—treated as
highest sin. To listen to your body, which knows
how freedom feels seen as rebellion—apostasy
and unbelief.

Dear unfree who've been told you are—

Unseating high-controlling churches and
people from your life and sinking into that
blessed Belovedness and freedom that's
yours will require a stirring of your
curiosity: sitting a little longer,
a little deeper, with questions.

Here's to letting lose the holy rebellion in
your bones. Here's to soaring and voicing like
the free they call "mad," for the very thing they
forbade—the curiosity of your voice, brain, body—is
the very thing that pulses your wings.

True freedom is being loved by a God
big enough to take our cries, questions, and doubts.
True freedom is not having all the answers
and knowing that's okay.

Your Thoughts

Sisterhood: I Am with Her

I am with her.

The one shouted down, made voiceless;
moving in the shadows, wounded and distrusting of
shiny Christian light. The one those closest to
the thundering shepherd pushed and drove away,
believing her anguished state is a bother to
their busy herdsman.

I am with her, who limps into gatherings with a
quivering heart and bruises, the most unseen.
Still, she shuffles into the sheepfold, hoping
today would be the day a kind hand offers support
for her disturbed gait, a tiny sign from the body
of Christ that she and her pain matters.

I am with her
Because we share a common thread of humanity.

I am not with those served by a system
that benefits from her silence and sidelining.
Those who stand by, refusing to pick a side.
Those who seek to destroy her soul
or idly watch as it slowly slips away.

I am with her,
a witness to her story. Adding my voice
in spaces that pretend she doesn't exist.
Lamenting as they try to compel her back
into the shadows.

Our Shepherd's words ring out.
Freedom.
Resurrection.
Life.
Peace.
Joy
Love.

I am with her,
not with those who war against her.[6]

Your Thoughts

Her Strength

The strength of a woman is not in how well
she adapts to a one-sided marriage
or endures a chronically immature connection.

Her strength is not in how sweet and respectful
she remains while disrespected and dishonored. It's not
in how she glows as she shrinks her needs and
expands her limits to accommodate endless
depleting demands "while keeping the faith."

The strength of a woman is not just in
her "Yes." It's also in her "No."

When she's unsafe, unseen, unheard—when
something needs to shift in the relationship, it's in
her boundaries; her giving herself permission to
acknowledge her needs and embrace her limitations;
her moving out of the way and letting her spouse
meet the consequences of his behaviors and
beliefs; her detaching from people and spaces
that are fiercer promoters of her relationship
than her worth and safety.

Ready or not, the tide is turning.

God's daughters embracing the truth
that they are just as worthy as the sons,
that they were not created to mop up after
the other gender: they are deserving of
dignity, honor, respect, loyalty, fidelity.
They are not less than or second-class
citizens, or an afterthought.

They are image bearers, co-heirs of the
gracious gift of life in Christ
and equal partners in
relationships.

The tidal wave is rising.

Your Thoughts

Safer

To those with strong feelings about people
Who've left the four walls of a church
building: be thankful you never had
to make the tough decision to protect
yourself from those you trusted most.

To those questioning the
genuineness of those who left the faith:
be grateful you've never known the
shattering of everything you held dear.

To those querying the sincerity of those
who left church because they didn't feel
like they belong: be glad you've never felt
entirely alone and unknown in the place
you should feel most at home.

To those amused by the sojourners still in the
desert, still trekking, still looking and searching:
be grateful your faith hasn't had to crawl
on its knees as you bled out.

It's a privilege. To be untouched,
to be oblivious of religious and
relational abuse and
resultant trauma.

We don't need hard places to have depth.
But we experience something extra when
we allow ourselves to sink into another's story
of hardship. When we listen, think, wander,
and explore. Together.

While unwanted or undeserved,
hard places can afford *all* a
unique and profound depth.
Because as we look into each other's eyes, we
discover, buried in their light, our own:
our human story.

To the querying, wandering, and pain-filled,
we can bear witness.

To the learning, those attempting to see life
through another's eyes, we can be
the substance that makes this world
better and safer for all.

Your Thoughts

Church Escape

Can churches be where women learn and
embrace how much God loves and keeps them
safe?

Can the sacredness of Christian gathering be the
healing pool from which the forgotten half of humanity
experiences the Living Water, is reminded they
matter more than the marital places they dwell?

Can Christians be the people who validate
and applaud the *imago Dei* in all, not just some?

Can church be known as a community that
affirms and fans the standard of love, not just when
the winds of community and belonging blow
outward to others, but also and especially when they
blow inward, settling deep down inside our bones,
for love for oneself instructs love for another?

Can church be where we all understand that women
who escape destructive marriages didn't do so at the
first whiff of a destructive mindset or action? Where we know
they stayed so long, gaze steady, hands busy, lungs filling up
with unhealth, doing the good work they were told
good Christian women do?

When she saw the crumbling, the haze in her gaze,
the shallowness of breath, the reality of her
life, her children, her sanity slowly slipping
despite her busy hands, when clarity called
her name—can the church trust she had all
along tried her best, but one person's best
is not enough when the finest from both
was required?

Can the church be where the wounded
don't have to escape to find
freedom and healing?

Your Thoughts

Fraudulent Religion

I was anxious, and they gave me more to do.
I was afraid; they said I lacked faith.
I was scared, and they said I was imagining it.
I was hurting, and they told me, "Come to church."
I had questions, and they labeled me a sinner.
I needed truth, and they called me a deserter.
As my soul bled out, they said to stop
staining the name of their god.

Controlling and exacting,
demanding and perfectionistic,
exploiting and two-faced,
a ruler with little to no mercy
for my struggle and pain
is the god they gave me.

Turns out what they handed me was
a counterfeit god. I was merely an apostate
of their fraudulent religion.

But Truth had always been with me; He was
the initiator and sustainer of the bubble
in my bones. He was the soft in the hard.
The rest in the straining. The shelter in
the storms. The calm in the anxiety.
The acceptance in the shame. The
steady in the alienation.

God is, as He always has
been in every breath, shallow
or deep, a steady, connecting
presence opening our eyes
to who He's always been and
who we always were and will be.

Your Thoughts

Abuser god

Some Christians believe most divorced people leave
behind a fabulous spouse and life, that they should have
just "persevered," "been a little more patient," "lowered
some expectations," "met their spouse halfway."

Some Christians worship an abuser god, a micro-manager
who exerts power and control over his creation,
a user who will exploit and abandon at will.

They believe in a god who needs to be placated and pleased*
with good deeds to stay close, one who says he loves but mostly
actively dislikes people.

They believe in a god who hurts his creation on purpose to help
them love him more, who is one way today
and another tomorrow
and can never be trusted to be constant.

They believe in a god who demands more than he'll ever give, at least
at a human-experience level, and expects everything in return.

We never rise above our beliefs, so these "Christians" do not understand
why a spouse escapes, because if she had really *tried*—the same way
they try with their god—then she would "love" up close and personal too,
even though it hurts, dysregulates, and breaks.

Toxic theology gives birth to toxic beliefs around relationships,
leads us to believe
we never deserve
to be safe and happy.

---

*For more on this topic, check out Krispin Mayfield's book, *Attached to God: A Practical Guide to Deeper Spiritual Experience*

Your Thoughts

In His Image

It is not "God created *Christians* in his own image."
It is "God created *humankind* in his own image."

Image-bearer is not a dignity reserved
for human beings who are Christians.

When we resolve this within
ourselves as Christians then perhaps those
who've borne the brunt of our other-ring,
who've been swept away by our
floods of indignity,
considered mere targets
of conversion and judgment,
instead of worthy, precious, and needed
shall feel safe in our presence.

When we understand all human beings
are created in the Image of God,
perhaps we'll also understand
why we are all accountable
and don't deserve special
privileges for existing
as human beings
who are Christians.

Your Thoughts

Not a Mistake

It's not a "mistake" when it's repeated often,
not a "tolerable quirk" when it hurts you,
not a "normal" way to relate when one person is
trounced, silenced, and cast aside,
not "your portion" when God said it's not,
not "what every man does" when Scripture is clear
what healthy looks like.

Some Christians say they love and then *do* the opposite
of love and consider their doing normal.

Let the abuser, rebellious and proud, call it normal or
whatever they want,
but you
do not have to believe
what they believe.

"No one who lives in him keeps on sinning. No one
who continues to sin has either seen him or known him.
Dear children, do not let anyone lead you astray. The
one who does what is right is righteous, just as he is
righteous. The one who does what is sinful is of the
devil, because the devil has been sinning from the
beginning. The reason the Son of God appeared
was to destroy the devil's work. No one who is
born of God will continue to sin, because God's
seed remains in them; they cannot go on sinning,
because they have been born of God. This is
how we know who the children of God are
and who the children of the devil are: Anyone
who does not do what is right is not God's
child, nor is anyone who does not love
their brother and sister."[8]

Your Thoughts

Her

I think of her
whose light dimmed.
Sadness wore her like a garment.

Whose husband, bright and charming, laid back
and sweet, buzzed in the busy, public limelight
of church service and volunteerism. Her, whose
private and uncomfortable marital tidbits were
shared without her consent as "testimony" by men
hungry for accolades and success. Her, who wilted
under the church's gaze, considered a blight to
a husband's ministry forays. Her, who stopped
attending church services, and nobody
paused to ask why, or when they did,
tongues never topped wagging.

I think about the women who didn't say much,
and when they did, nobody believed them.

I think about a church culture
that refuses to pursue the
counterculture ways of its Leader—
the One Who came to untie the binds and
set captives free.[7]

Your Thoughts

She

She is not lacking the
desire or willingness,
faith or muscle,
mercy or forgiveness,
love or devotion.

She is just tired of
saving him
fixing him
mothering him
defending him
regulating him
dying for him,
being his god.

She just wants to
breathe
discern
understand
grow
heal
thrive—
live in truth.

Your Thoughts

The Rupture

Your fight for sanity and wholeness
didn't
break the marriage.
Your spouse's
hardness of heart
and unrepentance
did.

To discern wickedness and unrepentance,
to diagnose its rotten guts and
recognize when life has been sucked out
instead of added in,
as a healthy marriage does,
is holy and sacred—
courage worthy to be celebrated.

Some Christians will summon a battle song and
stir up accusations and
label your labor of survival in a brutal environment,
your boundaries,
your loyalty to the ideals of love
as the cause of or contributor to the marriage
"breaking."

Lean in, seer of truth
and warrior of love;
you didn't
cause
the rupture, you
called it out.

Those who love you,
who are in allyship, know
the truth
and believe you.

Your Thoughts

Love Is

Love is not quick to punish
Love is not cruel
Love is not jealous
Love does not show off
Love is not cocky
Love does not behave itself unseemingly
Love is not self-serving
Love is not provoked to anger
Love does not nurse grievances
Love does not exalt wickedness.

Love rejoices in integrity
Love always shields and keeps from harm
Love always trusts
Love always hopes
Love always perseveres.

"Love is patient, love is kind. It does not envy,
it does not boast, it is not proud. It does not
dishonor others, it is not self-seeking,
it is not easily angered, it keeps no
record of wrongs. Love does
not delight in evil but rejoices
with the truth. It always
protects, always trusts,
always hopes, always
perseveres."[9]

Your Thoughts

Culture

Dear wife married to a man
who likes to pull the culture card
to make you accept his problematic
way of relating:[10]

It's not his heritage or way of life
that brings out the vile
that twists your
insides;
he does what he does because he
can.
To be toxic, entitled, and corrosive
is a choice he has made.
"It's my culture"
is an excuse
to keep up the ruse.

Does he treat his mom, siblings, and others
from his culture
the same way?
Does he do
the same things he does to you
at work,
with his colleagues,
friends,
or people he respects?
Does he tantrum
at church,
in front of his pastor,
when the pastor says something
he doesn't like?
Is this way of relating
consistent across all his relationships,
or exclusive to yours?

It's not culture. It's him,
doing what he does
because he can.

Harmful people find things to
baptize their vileness. Excuses
and "reasons" out of thin air to "explain"
why they are the way they are.

Do not believe their ruses and stories
to justify why exactly
they won't change.

Instead, believe yourself,
the patterns of what you see and feel,
the history
of how *safe* people
in your culture
think and act.

Your Thoughts

Wifehood Is Not a Death Sentence

"Wife" does not imply
inferiority
or caretaking
a nonfunctioning,
immature,
betraying,
abusive system
of relating.

Women are not receptacles
for entitled, corrosive
mindsets and behaviors.

A wife is a powerful, competent,
equal partner.

Wife, *you* are worthy of a gentle,
peaceful existence. You are worthy
of joy and happiness. You are worthy
of safety, loyalty, and faithfulness.
You are worthy
of hope,
of a bountiful future.

You did not sign up for prison time
when you said,
"I do."
You signed up for a healthy,
growing partnership
marked
by repentance
and fruit-bearing.

Your Thoughts

Watch Out

Watch out for those who tell you to accept a
rigid, forceful relationship,
who baptize it the "Biblical order."
Watch out when they say
to swim in anxiety and fear,
calling it "conviction" and "devotion."

Watch out
for those who ask you to ignore your emotions
and body, expecting you to make
an enemy
of those tender parts of you
that are good and holy.

Watch out for those who want you to dance in the house
of enslavement,
requiring quietness and niceness as
your personhood is expelled.

They call your ending "sanctification," the image of God
in you
abused and dying,
"becoming like Christ."

Watch out
when they call wrong right and right wrong,
when they turn away from questions and new information,
catastrophizing every assessment and critique.

Watch out for them,
for they will not lend their ears;
"too much grave smell," "too much grief and lamentation,"
is the tale the suffering and troubled are told when their
grief breaks the illusion of satiety, and pain can no longer
be contained in habituated piety.

Watch out for when they demand softness and sweetness
in the day of trouble and turmoil.
As if the day of the dirge
is less precious than the day of resurrection.

Watch for when they demand song and rejoicing
when their very ways contributed to numbness and
destruction.

Watch those whose hearts are distant and untouched
by the sting of your torment,
who bring potions and herbs
to anoint your wounds.

Watch out for those who have historically aligned themselves
to the preservation of institutions and systems—
who, still unchanged, want to sketch the maps to guide
shuffling wounded souls out of the desert to
shaded streams of healing.

Watch out for those who peddle a Christianity
devoid of empathy,
truth,
or justice. Whose eyes
are unseeing,
hearts
unfeeling.

Watch out for those who walk right past Jesus
as they jostle to maintain "a Biblical standard."

"'The Spirit of the Lord is on me, because he has anointed me to proclaim good news to the poor. He has sent me to proclaim freedom for the prisoners and recovery of sight for the blind, to set the oppressed free, to proclaim the year of the Lord's favor.' Then he rolled up the scroll, gave it back to the attendant and sat down. The eyes of everyone in the synagogue were fastened on him. He began by saying to them, 'Today this scripture is fulfilled in your hearing.'"[11]

"The Son is the image of the invisible God, the firstborn over all creation. For in him all things were created: things in heaven and on earth, visible and invisible, whether thrones or powers or rulers or authorities; all things have been created through him and for him. He is before all things, and in him all things hold together. And he is the head of the body, the church; he is the beginning and the firstborn from among the dead, so that in everything he might have the supremacy. For God was pleased to have all his fullness dwell in him, and through him to reconcile to himself all things, whether things on earth or things in heaven, by making peace through his blood, shed on the cross."[12]

Your Thoughts

Silenced Prayer

Pain silenced my prayer,
taught me what prayer was not.

Earnest words—long and winding.
Anxious pleading—begging and beseeching.
Washing my parts in a daily ritual of self-flagellation.
Burying my quivering dysregulation with more to-dos.
Baptizing all these orchestrations.
"Spending time with God in prayer."

Pain burst through the door.
Uninvited and interruptive.
Licking my insides with fire,
blanketing my brain with strange confusion.
Holding and imprisoning me in my own body.

Pain incinerated my good-girl prayers and hopes
and silenced all the words I'd ever known.

Collapsed, all I had was stillness
fog, tears, sighs—wordlessness
from a full heart.

I learned communion with my Creator
isn't just words or earnestness.
It's not
like a peel tossed onto pavement—
unsure when I'll slide,
taking down all my religion with me.

Communion is quiet and tender,
without effort, pushing, or lather.

Communion
is the quiet,
as where pain is,
God is too.

Your Thoughts

Goodwilled

"Good-willed" couples
can wound each other
and say hurtful things.

They can be immature,
have trauma and unhealthy
coping behaviors.

But the "good" part of "good-willed"
will take the lead more often than not.

Spouses with good will
are familiar with the limits of love.
They are accountable, not an excuse pit.

They hug truth and embrace reality.
They don't cultivate separate public and private personas.

Spouses carrying good in their hearts
listen to and receive others' viewpoints.

Their souls are kind and hold empathy.

They wrestle and learn, commit and follow through,
and bear long-term fruit.

Spouses familiar with the boundaries of love
are not a stone wall
where all forward movement
and improvements
go to die.
They don't give promises of change
only to return to their vomit
tomorrow.

Hardheartedness and remorselessness,
as an underlying, persistent pattern
of relating, are alien
to the good-willed
spouse.

Your Thoughts

The Baseline

Feeling as "one" in marriage,
approaching hard things as a team,
being aware of what's theirs to carry
and what is not—
these are not big asks.

Happiness and being valued and cherished,
partnership and feeling safe in hard conversations,
eyes-lighting-up-like-the-sun
and tender connection to the loved one—
these are basics, not something women
should have to fight or beg for.

It must feel safe
to be with her mate.
A healthy baseline
should be accessible to both in the marriage.
When it's not, the answer is not
to tell her—to make her—ask smaller.

Your Thoughts

Peeling Away

"You don't owe me anything."

The words felt whispered from heaven after therapy,
a session in which I was reminded and affirmed about
the kindness of God.

If you have a people-pleasing disposition,
born of deep hurts
where keeping folk regulated was
what worked
and how you belonged—not owing anything*
to anyone
can be a confusing ache of contradiction.

It is welcome like the cooling breeze on skin
that has been blasted away in a fiery furnace.
It is as grand of an arrival
as a second set of hands
bursting from ribbed sides
one lazy Saturday morning.

The thought
that you owe nothing
can leave you relaxed—
and completely disoriented.

But an anchor all the same,
as gradually,
studiously,
at times ferally—
you peel away, like old dirty band-aids, those who want you
to pay
in order to belong.

Now you know:
the pay-to-belong crew
represents Him
not at all.

*Anything beyond normal decency that respects the image of God
in another.

Your Thoughts

Co-Regulating with Christ

Sitting in the presence
of Kindness, Love, Compassion
gives me the courage to face my fears,
disruptions and dysregulations.

Christ's kindness
is the roadmap
to giving kindness
to myself.

From His richness where
I don't fight to be loved,
to belong,

I pour into my empty cup

choosing kindness
over frustration
for myself.[13]

Your Thoughts

The African Lament: Home

I think of siblings, who descend from a shared lineage.
I think of our ancestors who once knew puffy clouds
who sang, danced, twirled and
called each other by name under bright African skies.

An American of Kenyan descent, I can jump on a plane
when the land of my sunny rooting calls my name,
for I know exactly where my "pin" plants
in the vast lands of Africa.

Mercy the ancestors who came in shackles and ships,
ripped from freedom, rays and blue skies, their blood
running in the veins of their offspring repositioned
in America, far from the land of their ancestors' birth.

We walk in this world looking for the pin on a map
that would tell us, "Home is here."

Not a plane ride, not a memory,
but a Belovedness, right here and now.
A longing for the ending of longings.
A soul whisper that reminds us of belonging.
A place called Beloved, Him making home
with us here.

Your Thoughts

The Choice

Your questions and concerns
will not serve those who want to
maintain power and privilege
over you.

When your current position benefits them,
your growing awareness, capacity to reflect,
and desire to use your voice will neither
be welcomed nor celebrated.

The truth is, no colonizer enjoys the day
when the people start inspecting and
disrobing the systems and structures that
keep them in place.

Examining the composition and asking the questions,
voicing concerns and expecting multiplication,
will invite deflection,
minimization,
denial and justification
for every mindset and deed.

Therefore, choose wisely and safely
where your energy will best be spent.

Your own safety, health, progress, and strength—
or fighting to change those who are most dedicated
to keeping you where
you no longer want to be.

Your Thoughts

About the Author

Ngina Otiende was born and raised in Kenya, a beautiful East African nation that wraps its golden arms around the equator. She is married to Tommy, and for the last 12 years, they have made the United States their home. You can find Ngina writing about liberation, hope, and health in marriage at IntentionalToday.com, Facebook @IntentionalToday, and Instagram @nginaotiende.

Website: IntentionalToday.com
Facebook: @IntentionalToday
Instagram: @nginaotiende

Notes

1. In a Facebook post from June 1, 2023, Sheila Gregoire, a popular author and podcaster, shared her frustration over commenters who say her daughter (a fellow author and podcaster) gets too passionate and loud about things. Sheila's husband, however, a frequent guest on the podcast, is more passionate and blunt than their daughter, but nobody complains about him or other male guests on the podcast when they get angry and harsh in their commentaries and observations. Last accessed June 6, 2023. <https://www.facebook.com/Sheila.Gregoire.Books/posts/pfbid02p9nKyzL4WUw5wvaUKbvYtf8cDYMe4R2BQRRdz6apfdte1WzBcnqerdQmjKXkvyWfl>

2. Google's English dictionary is provided by Oxford Languages.

3. Genesis 2:23.

4. I highly recommend Marg Mowczko <https://margmowczko.com/> for theology articles on mutuality and the equality of men and women in Christian marriage and ministry.

5. This poem was inspired by Andrew J. Bauman's blog post, "Egalitarianism vs. Complementarianism: What about Submission?" <https://andrewjbauman.com/submission/> Last accessed June 5, 2023. Andrew is a licensed mental health counselor.

6. If you are *her* or know *her*, there are communities with wide open arms waiting to hold you and walk with you. You are not alone. Here are just a few of them:

   • Wilderness to WILD with Sarah McDugal
   • Abi Akinola
   • Patrick Weaver Ministries
   • MaryEllen Bream/Hope for Hurting Wives
   • Flying Free with Natalie Hoffman
   • The Life-Saving Divorce with Gretchen Baskerville
   • Held and Healed with Heather Elizabeth
   • Thriving Forward with Emily Anderson

   Also Consider
   • Bare Marriage with Sheila Gregoire
   • Black Liturgies/Cole Arthur Riley
   • Sarah Jackson Coaching

Explore each of these and consider connecting. You will find truth-walking, compassion, kindness, and strength in increasing measure all waiting for you. You are not alone.

7. *The Great Sex Rescue* and *She Deserves Better* by Sheila Gregoire, Rebecca Lindenbach, and Joanna Sawatsky (Baker Books, Michigan) explore in detail, using research, how toxic Christian teachings have actively set up systems of harm, not health.

8. 1 John 3:6-10.

9. 1 Corinthians 13:4-7

10. I receive questions from non-African women married to African men asking, "Is X behavior a cultural thing?" They will go on to describe juvenile, coercive mindset and behaviors. Different cultures have their own propensity towards patriarchy and male entitlement, and my Kenyan culture is no different. That said, not every African man runs on male patriarchy or calls evil good. Some do. Others don't. And many choose to grow and bear good fruit.

11. Luke 4:16-21.

12. Colossians 1:15-20.

13. Dr. Virginia Holema in her article "Thrive In 5-Co-Regulation (Relational)" defines co-regulation this way: "When our fight, flight, freeze response is triggered by frightening circumstances or our own thoughts, we often need the support of 'co-regulation' to regain a sense of safety and calm. Co-regulation happens when two nervous systems get in sync. While systems can move into co-dysregulation, with each one heightening the alarm of the other, one 'non-anxious presence' can help the other's alarmed nervous system find calm." <https://www.wesleyan.org/thrive-in-5-co-regulation-relational> Last accessed June 2, 2023. For the Christian, Christ is the "non-anxious presence," and we can accept His invitation to settle into His calm and safety. His peace and love and compassion becomes our path to regulating the stress, shame, or fears in our own bodies as we give to ourselves what we have received from Christ.

www.ingramcontent.com/pod-product-compliance
Lightning Source LLC
Chambersburg PA
CBHW070758050426
42452CB00012B/2393